A **Literature Kit**™ F O R

Fantastic Mr Fox

By Roald Dahl

Written by Michelle Jensen

GRADES 3-4

Classroom Complete Press

P.O. Box 19729

San Diego, CA 92159

Tel: 1-800-663-3609 | Fax: 1-800-663-3608

Email: service@classroomcompletepress.com

www.classroomcompletepress.com

ISBN – 13: 978-1-77167-244-3

© 2015

Critical Thinking Skills

Fantastic Mr Fox

Skills For Critical Thinking	Section Questions										Writing Tasks	Graphic Organizers
	1	2	3-4	5-6	7-8	9-10	11-12	13-14	15-16	17-18		
LEVEL 1 — Remembering												
• Identify Story Elements		✓	✓	✓	✓	✓	✓		✓	✓	✓	✓
• Recall Details	✓	✓	✓	✓	✓	✓	✓	✓	✓	✓	✓	✓
• Match	✓	✓		✓	✓	✓	✓			✓		
• Sequence Events								✓		✓		✓
LEVEL 2 — Understanding												
• Compare & Contrast	✓	✓		✓	✓	✓	✓		✓		✓	
• Summarize		✓	✓	✓			✓	✓		✓	✓	✓
• State Main Idea					✓		✓	✓		✓		✓
• Describe	✓	✓	✓	✓		✓	✓	✓	✓	✓	✓	✓
• Classify			✓		✓	✓						
LEVEL 3 — Applying												
• Plan		✓	✓			✓	✓				✓	
• Interview								✓			✓	
• Infer Outcomes	✓		✓	✓	✓		✓	✓		✓		
LEVEL 4 — Analysing												
• Draw Conclusions	✓	✓	✓	✓	✓	✓	✓		✓	✓	✓	✓
• Identify Supporting Evidence	✓	✓	✓	✓	✓	✓	✓	✓	✓	✓	✓	✓
• Motivations	✓	✓	✓	✓		✓	✓	✓	✓	✓	✓	✓
• Identify Cause & Effect	✓			✓	✓	✓	✓					
LEVEL 5 — Evaluating												
• State & Defend An Opinion	✓	✓	✓	✓	✓	✓	✓	✓	✓	✓	✓	✓
• Make Judgements	✓			✓	✓		✓	✓		✓	✓	
LEVEL 6 — Creating												
• Predict	✓		✓	✓	✓	✓	✓	✓				
• Design	✓			✓							✓	
• Create								✓			✓	
• Imagine Alternatives		✓		✓	✓	✓	✓			✓	✓	

Based on Bloom's Taxonomy

Contents

TEACHER GUIDE

- Assessment Rubric 4
- How Is Our **Literature Kit**™ Organized? 5
- Graphic Organizer 6
- Bloom's Taxonomy for Reading Comprehension 7
- Teaching Strategies 7
- Summary of the Story 8
- Vocabulary 9

STUDENT HANDOUTS

- Spotlight on Roald Dahl 10
- Chapter Questions
  - *Chapter 1* 11
  - *Chapter 2* 14
  - *Chapters 3-4* 17
  - *Chapters 5-6* 20
  - *Chapters 7-8* 23
  - *Chapters 9-10* 26
  - *Chapters 11-12* 29
  - *Chapters 13-14* 32
  - *Chapters 15-16* 35
  - *Chapters 17-18* 38
- Writing Tasks 41
- Word Search 44
- Comprehension Quiz 45

EASY MARKING™ ANSWER KEY 47

GRAPHIC ORGANIZERS 53

✔ **6 BONUS Activity Pages!** Additional worksheets for your students

Download a digital copy for use with your projection system or interactive whiteboard

FREE!

- Go to our website: **www.classroomcompletepress.com/bonus**
- Enter item CC2316
- Enter pass code CC2316D for Activity Pages.

© CLASSROOM COMPLETE PRESS   **Fantastic Mr Fox CC2316**

Assessment Rubric

Fantastic Mr Fox

Student's Name: __________

Assignment: __________

Level: __________

	Level 1	Level 2	Level 3	Level 4
Comprehension of Novel	Demonstrates a limited understanding of the novel	Demonstrates some understanding of the novel	Demonstrates a considerable understanding of the novel	Demonstrates a thorough understanding of the novel
Content • Information and details relevant to focus	Elements are incomplete; key details missing	Some elements are complete; details missing	All required elements are complete; key details contain some description	All required elements are complete; enough description for clarity
Style • Effective word choice and originality • Precise language	Little variety in word choice. Language vague and imprecise	Some variety in word choice. Language somewhat vague and imprecise	Good variety in word choice. Language precise and quite descriptive	Writer's voice is apparent throughout. Excellent choice of words. Precise language
Conventions • Spelling, language, capitalization, punctuation	Errors seriously interfere with the writer's purpose	Repeated errors in mechanics and usage	Some errors in convention	Few errors in convention

STRENGTHS:

WEAKNESSES:

NEXT STEPS:

Fantastic Mr Fox CC2316

Teacher Guide

Our resource has been created for ease of use by both TEACHERS and STUDENTS alike.

Introduction

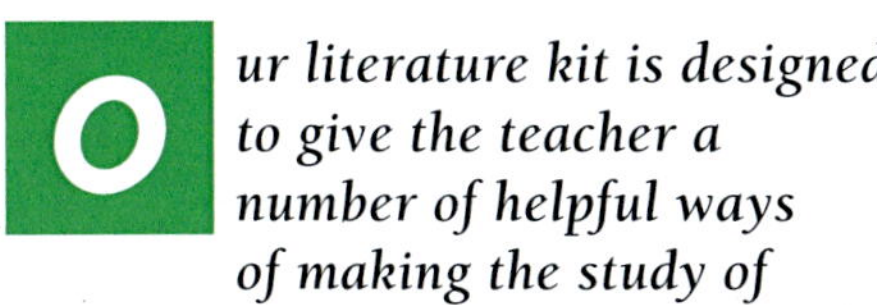

Our literature kit is designed to give the teacher a number of helpful ways of making the study of this novel a more enjoyable and profitable experience for the students. Our guide features a number of useful and flexible components, from which the teacher can choose. It is not expected that all of the activities will be completed.

One advantage to this approach to the study of a novel is that the student can work at his or her own speed, and the teacher can assign activities that match the student's abilities.

Our literature kit divides the novel by chapters and features reading comprehension and vocabulary questions. Themes include survival, family and friend relationships, and problem solving. Fantastic Mr Fox allows students to appreciate how to solve problems and how difficulties in life often make us stronger or improve our lives.

How Is Our Literature Kit™ Organized?

STUDENT HANDOUTS

Chapter Activities (*in the form of reproducible worksheets*) make up the majority of this resource. For each group of chapters, there are BEFORE YOU READ activities and AFTER YOU READ activities.

- The BEFORE YOU READ activities prepare students for reading by setting a purpose for reading. They stimulate background knowledge and experience, and guide students to make connections between what they know and what they will learn. Important concepts and vocabulary from the chapter(s) are also presented.
- The AFTER YOU READ activities check students'

comprehension and extend their learning. Students are asked to give thoughtful consideration of the text through creative and evaluative short-answer questions and journal prompts.

Six **Writing Tasks** and three **Graphic Organizers** are included to further develop students' critical thinking and writing skills, and analysis of the text. (*See page 6 for suggestions on using the Graphic Organizers.*) The **Assessment Rubric** (*page 4*) is a useful tool for evaluating students' responses to the Writing Tasks and Graphic Organizers.

PICTURE CUES

This resource contains three main types of pages, each with a different purpose and use. A **Picture Cue** at the top of each page shows, at a glance, what the page is for.

Teacher Guide
- Information and tools for the teacher

Student Handout
- Reproducible worksheets and activities

Easy Marking™ Answer Key
- Answers for student activities

EASY MARKING™ ANSWER KEY

Marking students' worksheets is fast and easy with this **Answer Key**. Answers are listed in columns—just line up the column with its corresponding worksheet, as shown, and see how every question matches up with its answer!

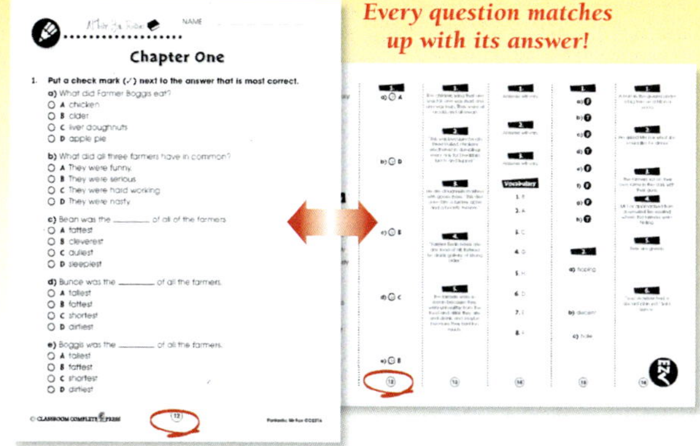

1, 2, 3
Graphic Organizers

The three **Graphic Organizers** included in this Literature Kit™ are especially suited to a study of *Fantastic Mr Fox.* Below are suggestions for using each organizer in your classroom, or they may also be adapted to suit the individual needs of your students. The organizers can be used on a projection system or interactive whiteboard in teacher-led activities, small group activities, and/or photocopied for use as student worksheets. To evaluate students' responses to any of the organizers, you may wish to use the **Assessment Rubric** (on page 4).

CHARACTER SKETCH

Students will draw out details about the character of Mr Fox by adding facts and quotes to the following character sketch. In the graphic organizer, there is space to identify many characteristics and values held by Mr Fox, including: his loves, strengths, weaknesses, thoughts and dreams. This format can be used to help draw information out on other characters as well.

Found on Page 53.

SUMMARY SENTENCE SANDWICH

Using this graphic organizer, students can easily organize their facts from the story into a Topic Sentence (ie: Mr Fox is a fantastic Fox). Students will use facts from the story to add layers of detail and build a summary paragraph to show how Mr Fox is fantastic. Finally, they will conclude the paragraph with a reworded statement.

Found on Page 54.

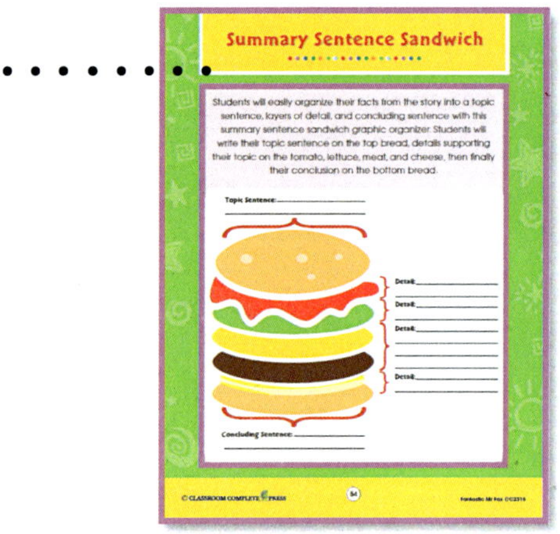

PLOT DIAGRAM

Using this graphic organizer, students are able to gather the key points to plot development: introduction, rising action, climax, falling action, and conclusion. Students are encouraged to write down quotes to help them find facts in the story.

Found on Page 55.

Bloom's Taxonomy* for Reading Comprehension

The activities in this resource engage and build the full range of thinking skills that are essential for students' reading comprehension. Based on the six levels of thinking in Bloom's Taxonomy, questions are given that challenge students to not only recall what they have read, but to move beyond this to understand the text through higher-order thinking. By using higher-order skills of applying, analyzing, evaluating and creating, students become active readers, drawing more meaning from the text, and applying and extending their learning in more sophisticated ways.

This **Literature Kit™**, therefore, is an effective tool for any Language Arts program. Whether it is used in whole or in part, or adapted to meet individual student needs, this resource provides teachers with the important questions to ask, inspiring students' interest and creativity, and promoting meaningful learning.

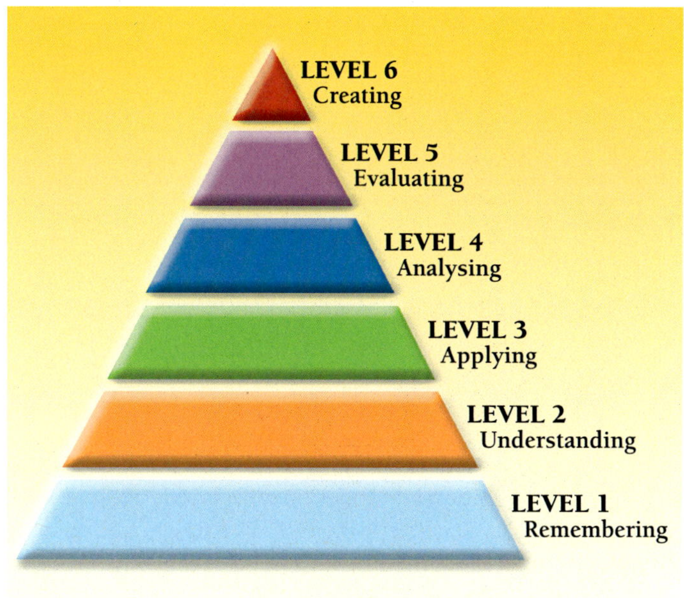

**BLOOM'S TAXONOMY:
6 LEVELS OF THINKING**

**Bloom's Taxonomy is a widely used tool by educators for classifying learning objectives, and is based on the work of Benjamin Bloom.*

Teaching Strategies — WHOLE-CLASS, SMALL GROUP AND INDEPENDENT STUDY

This study guide contains the following activities:

Before Reading Activities: themes are introduced and thought-provoking questions put forward for the students to consider.

Vocabulary Activities: new and unfamiliar words are introduced and reviewed.

After Reading Questions: the first part of this section includes short answer questions dealing with the content of the text. The second part features questions that are more open-ended and feature concepts from the higher order of Bloom's Taxonomy.

Writing Tasks: creative writing assignments based on Bloom's Taxonomy that relate to the plot of the particular chapters.

A **comprehension quiz** is also included comprised of multiple-choice, true/false and short-answer questions.

Graphic Organizers: three full-page reproducible sheets have been included and can be used for teaching purposes throughout the text.

Bonus Sheets are also available online.

The study guide can be used in a variety of ways in the classroom depending on the needs of the students and teacher. The teacher may choose to use an independent reading approach with students capable of working independently. It also works well with small groups, with most of the lessons being quite easy to follow. Finally, in other situations, teachers will choose to use it with their entire class.

Teachers may wish to have their students keep a daily reading log so that they might record their daily progress and reflections.

Fantastic Mr Fox CC2316

Summary of the Story

Fantastic *Mr Fox* is a story about a fox providing for his family. Mr Fox lives in a den in the country near three very unusual farmers. He gets his food from the farms of these greedy and disgusting farmers. Naturally, the farmers are not happy; they don't like the fox stealing from them. The three farmers decide to catch the fox and kill him. Then the action begins with the farmers trying to catch the fox by hiding outside his den. Mr Fox is a very careful fox but he is almost killed by the farmers.

The farmers become more and more desperate to kill the fox. They try everything from rifles, to diggers, to dynamite. Mr Fox uses all his skills and intelligence trying to outwit them. In order to avoid the farmers, Mr Fox and his family dig farther into the hill. They meet with their neighbors, fellow diggers under the hill. Mr Fox digs underground tunnels that allow him and his neighbors—the badgers and rabbits—to get food and drink, while staying safely underground.

In the end, Mr Fox outsmarts the three farmers and the farmers end up looking even more ridiculous. Mr Fox shows how important it is to 'stop and think of a plan' and to work with others. It is a funny story about survival, the importance of family and friends, and problem-solving.

Suggestions for Further Reading

OTHER BOOKS BY ROALD DAHL

James and the Giant Peach © 1961

Charlie and the Chocolate Factory © 1964

The Twits © 1980

George's Marvelous Medicine © 1981

The Witches © 1983

Matilda © 1988

OTHER RECOMMENDED RESOURCES

Richard Atwater, **Mr. Popper's Penguins** © 1938

E.B. White, **Stuart Little** © 1945

E.B. White, **Charlotte's Web** © 1952

Beverly Cleary, **The Mouse and the Motorcycle** © 1965

Beverly Cleary, **Socks** © 1973

Beverly Cleary, **Ralph S. Mouse** © 1982

Avi, **Poppy** © 1995

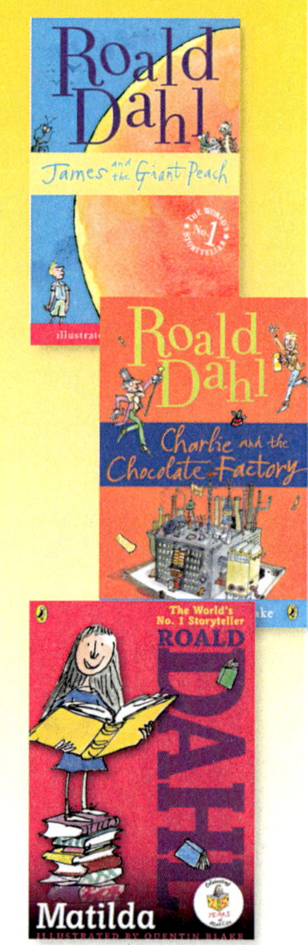

List of Vocabulary

CHAPTER 1
• nasty • enormously • smothered • pot-bellied • disgusting • beastly • cleverest • crooks

CHAPTER 2
• plump • creep • rage • lurking • 'dang and blast' • lousy • guts • blighter • decent • crafty

CHAPTERS 3 TO 4
• reeks • poisonous • cocky • crouched • twitched • rustling • pricked • murky • glint • tattered
• dozed • scrape • scrunch • fainter • 'phew'

CHAPTERS 5 TO 6
• cross • swig • boil • caterpillar • murderous • brutal • desperate • maniacs • jeered • furious
• obstinate

CHAPTERS 7 TO 8
• heck • crater • rage • declared • swore • solemn • oath • fetch • miserable • midget • sickly
• snatch • headlamps • hatchets • pistols • staring

CHAPTERS 9 TO 10
• dash • undefeated • courageous • marvelous • peek • ducked • a shriek • prancing
• Hallelujah • trough • lapped • plumpest • flick • jiffy

CHAPTERS 11 TO 12
• exploding • bursting • spluttered • tunnelled • plucking • whacking • churgle • chaos
• tease • galore

CHAPTERS 13 TO 14
• terrific pace • gaped • overwhelmed • proclaimed • grub • prowling • saliva • morsels • twerp
• loot • heap • dotty • frump • swipe • laid

CHAPTERS 15 TO 16
• sharp • saucy • pitch • tremendous • cellar • fiery • gurgled • poached • poppycock

CHAPTERS 17 TO 18
• glorious • impudent • hollowed • amid • ravenous • succulent • belch • courtesy • colossal
• famished • dash

Roald Dahl

Roald Dahl wrote many children's books. He once was asked why he wrote children's books, and he said: "I never get any protests from children. All you get are giggles of mirth and squirms of delight. I know what children like."

Roald Dahl led an extraordinary life. He was born in Landaff Wales on September 13, 1916, of Norwegian parents. Roald's father and sister died when Roald was 4 years old. His mother had to raise 6 children on her own. He loved his mother very much and based the grandmother in the story *The Witches* on his mother's personality.

What Roald Dahl didn't like was boarding school. He didn't like living away from home. He also didn't like the brutal discipline system used at the boarding schools. When he graduated, he applied to work with Shell Oil Company because he wanted to work and travel to exotic locations. He was able to live an exciting life working for Shell in East Africa. When World War II started, Roald Dahl volunteered as a fighter pilot in North Africa for the Royal Air Force. In 1942, he was injured and sent to work at the British Embassy in Washington D.C. It was while he was in Washington, that he started to write short stories.

Roald Dahl's life was full of much excitement, but also many tragedies. Roald Dahl's attitude when faced with life's problems was to roll up his sleeves and work on a solution. The father in the book *Fantastic Mr Fox*, has the same attitude. Roald Dahl's first wife suffered strokes during her first pregnancy. In response, Roald Dahl developed an exercise plan and speech therapy program for her to help her recover. When his son was 4 years old, he was hit by a car and suffered a brain injury. Roald Dahl worked with doctors to develop a shunt to remove extra liquid from the brain. Roald Dahl also had a rare blood disorder. He set up a fund to research cures and treatments for blood disorders. Roald Dahl uses exaggeration, irony, sarcasm and pathos in his children's stories.

Did You Know?

- His first published story was *Shot Down Over Libya*. It told of his experiences during World War II and was published on August 1, 1942.
- He wrote the screenplays for the movies *Chitty Chitty Bang Bang* and *You Only Live Twice*.
- Many of his stories have been turned into their own movies, like *James and the Giant Peach*, *Charlie and the Chocolate Factory*, and even *Fantastic Mr Fox*.

Chapter One

Answer the questions in full sentences.

1. The book is called: *Fantastic Mr Fox*. What do you know about foxes?

   a) Where do they live?______________________________

   ____

   b) What do they eat?________________________________

   ____

   c) Who are their enemies?___________________________

   ____

   d) What would make a fox FANTASTIC?__________________

   ____

Vocabulary **Fill in the blanks with a word(s) from the list.**

nasty	enormously	smothered	pot-bellied
disgusting	beastly	cleverest	crooks

1. Goose-liver doughnuts! That's ______________.

2. I would prefer doughnuts ______________ in icing.

3. He ate so much his stomach grew ______________ large!

4. "They are ______________! They called each other ______________ names."

5. "They are also ______________: they charged me $40.00 for a glass of water!"

6. "Some people have cats, some have dogs, but I have a ______________ pig for a pet," Inez explained.

7. Cats are sly, dogs are smart, but pigs are the ______________ of all."

NAME: _______________________

Chapter One

1. Put a check mark (✓) next to the answer that is most correct.

a) What did Farmer Boggis eat?
- ○ **A** chicken
- ○ **B** cider
- ○ **C** liver doughnuts
- ○ **D** apple pie

b) What did all three farmers have in common?
- ○ **A** They were funny.
- ○ **B** They were serious.
- ○ **C** They were hard working.
- ○ **D** They were nasty.

c) Bean was the ___________ of all of the farmers.
- ○ **A** fattest
- ○ **B** cleverest
- ○ **C** dullest
- ○ **D** sleepiest

d) Bunce was the ___________ of all the farmers.
- ○ **A** tallest
- ○ **B** fattest
- ○ **C** shortest
- ○ **D** dirtiest

e) Boggis was the ___________ of all the farmers.
- ○ **A** tallest
- ○ **B** fattest
- ○ **C** shortest
- ○ **D** dirtiest

Chapter One

Answer each question with a full sentence.

1. What did the children sing about the 3 farmers?

   ____

   ____

2. Why was farmer Boggis so fat? Find a quote from the chapter to prove your answer.

   ____

   ____

3. Why did farmer Bunce have a 'beastly temper'? Find a quote from the chapter to prove your answer.

   ____

   ____

4. Why was farmer Bean so thin? Find a quote from the chapter to prove your answer.

   ____

   ____

5. Why are the farmers so mean? Find hints from the chapter to prove your answer.

   ____

   ____

In the story, the three farmers have lots of money, food, and good farms. However, they don't seem very happy. What do you think will make the farmers happy? What makes you happy?

NAME: _______________________

Chapter Two

Answer the questions in full sentences.

1. What is the SETTING for this story so far?

____

____

2. In the song the children sing about the farmers, what do you think made them call the farmers 'crooks'?

____

3. How do farmers often feel about foxes? Why?

____

____

Vocabulary — Match the words on the left with its meaning on the right with a straight line.

1	lousy	sly	A
2	crafty	bad	B
3	creep	crawl slowly	C
4	rage	move to	D
5	lurking	pull apart	E
6	approached	good	F
7	rip	very mad	G
8	decent	hide and watch	H

Chapter Two

1. **(Circle)** **T** if the statement is **TRUE** or **F** if it is **FALSE**.

T F **a)** Mr and Mrs Fox had 2 kids.

T F **b)** The farmers hated Mr Fox.

T F **c)** Farmer Bunce knew where Mr Fox lived.

T F **d)** Farmer Bean came up with a plan to get Mr Fox.

T F **e)** The Fox could see the farmers in the dark.

T F **f)** Boggis was the leader for the farmers.

T F **g)** The farmers spoke respectfully to each other.

T F **h)** The farmers plan to shoot Mr Fox tomorrow night.

2. **Circle the correct word that would make the following sentences true.**

a) "So every night each of them would take his shotgun and hide in a dark place somewhere on his own farm, **hoping / hopping** to catch the robber."

b) "You've never had a **descent / decent** plan yet," said Bunce.

c) "Tomorrow night we will all hide outside the **hole / whole** where the fox lives."

Fantastic Mr Fox CC2316

NAME: __________________

Chapter Two

Answer each question with a full sentence.

1. Describe the home of the Fox family.

2. How did Mr Fox decide what food to get his family?

3. What did the farmers do to try to stop the fox each night?

4. How did Mr Fox stop from being shot every night?

5. "They were not men who like to give anything away". What do we know about the personalities of the farmers from this quote?

6. Find a quote from the story that proves the farmers have already tried to catch and kill Mr Fox.

Journaling Prompt

Some animals and insects are pests to us. Are they being bad from their point of view? Write a journal entry as if you were 'a pest', explaining your actions.

Chapters Three to Four

Word List

- cocky
- crouched
- doze
- glint
- murky
- phew
- poisonous
- pricked
- reeks
- rustling
- scrape
- scrunch
- tattered
- twitched

Across

2. Toxic.
6. Noise of movement in trees.
8. Dark and hard to see.
10. A light sleep.
12. To take off a top layer.

Down

1. Over confident.
2. Mr Fox tuned his ears in.
3. Squished.
4. Ragged.
5. A small quick movement.
7. A little light reflected off metal.
9. Smells really badly.
11. Stooped down.
13. A sound of relief.

Chapters Three to Four

1.   Fill in each blank with the correct words from the chapters.

a) "I can smell those goons a mile away. I can even smell one from the other. Boggis gives off a filthy stink of rotten __________. Bunce reeks of ___________, and as for Bean, the fumes of ___________ hang around him like poisonous gases."

b) "One of them __________ a flashlight on the hole, and there on the ground, in the circle of light, half in and half out of the hole, lay the poor ___________ bloodstained remains of…a fox's tail."

c) "There was no food for the foxes that night, and soon the children __________ off. Then Mrs Fox dozed off. But Mr Fox couldn't sleep because of the pain in the ___________ of his tail."

d) "Suddenly there was an especially loud __________ above their heads and the sharp end of the shovel came right through the __________. The sight of this __________ thing seemed to have an __________ effect upon Mr Fox."

2. Number the events from ❶ to ❻ in the order they occurred in these chapters.

a) Mr Fox was shot in the tail.

b) A shovel broke through the roof of the fox den.

c) The farmers hid in the woods outside the fox den.

d) The farmers started to dig into the hill.

e) The whole fox family started to dig deeper into the hill.

f) The little fox children fell asleep hungry.

Chapters Three to Four

Answer each question with a full sentence.

1. An author often hints about something that is going to happen. This is called 'foreshadowing'. Find a quote that hints to Mr Fox going to face danger on his hunt.

   ____

   ____

2. Why would Mr Fox be "especially careful coming out of his den?"

   ____

   ____

3. What 3 senses does Mr Fox use when going out to hunt?

   ____

4. How does Mr Fox react when he loses his tail?

   ____

5. What causes Mrs Fox to tell her children: "Your father is a fantastic fox."

   ____

   ____

6. What 4 ways is the Fox family a strong family?

   ____

   ____

Journaling Prompt

Every family faces emergencies in the home. Describe the plan you have with your family to safely leave your home in case of an emergency: like a fire. If your family does not already have a plan, make one up for them.

NAME: _______________________

Chapters Five to Six

Answer the questions in complete sentences.

1. In the last chapter, Mrs Fox said: "Your father is a fantastic fox." Why is Mr Fox fantastic?

   ____

   ____

2. What do you think the farmers will do next?

   ____

   ____

3. What do you think Mr Fox will do next?

   ____

   ____

Vocabulary **Circle the word that would best finish each sentence.**

1. Bunce was very__________.

   a) cross   **b)** jeered   **c)** boil

2. Bean was __________: he wanted to kill Mr Fox.

   a) furious **b)** murderous **c)** brutal

3. The farmers were __________ to try anything!

   a) divided   **b)** desperate **c)** obstinate

4. Bean tried to use his __________ to dig the fox out.

   a) swig   **b)** brutal   **c)** caterpillar

Chapters Five to Six

1. **Circle** **T** if the statement is **TRUE** or **F** if it is **FALSE**.

   T F **a)** The farmers dug all night.

   T F **b)** Bunce couldn't hear very well.

   T F **c)** Bean thought of using 'mechanical shovels'.

   T F **d)** The farmers carefully protected the trees while digging.

   T F **e)** "Dig for your lives," said Mrs Fox.

   T F **f)** The farmers stopped digging at lunch.

   T F **g)** The farmers were calm and logical.

   T F **h)** The land looked like a volcano after digging all day.

   T F **i)** The townspeople cheered the farmers digging.

2. **Put a check mark (✓) next to the answer that is most correct.**

   a) One of the things in Bean's ear holes is:

   ○ **A** dirt.

   ○ **B** chewing gum.

   ○ **C** candies.

   ○ **D** dead fleas.

   b) The townspeople 'jeer' at the farmers because they are:

   ○ **A** digging up the ground.

   ○ **B** funny looking.

   ○ **C** acting like crazy men.

   ○ **D** dirty and stinky.

NAME: _______________

Chapters Five to Six

Answer each question with a full sentence.

1. Why are the farmers 'very tired and cross'?

____

____

2. In Chapter 3, Bean said to dig the fox out. Boggis said: "Now you're talking sense." But in Chapter 5, what does Boggis say about it?

____

____

3. Why do you think Boggis and Bunce try Bean's ideas?

____

____

4. What is a bad side effect of the farmers using the diggers?

____

____

5. Why is Chapter 6 called 'The Race'?

____

____

Journaling Prompt

The farmers are not thinking ahead. They are just jumping into action. Can you think of a time when you just 'acted' without thinking it through? Describe what happened.

 Before You Read

Chapters Seven to Eight

Answer the questions in full sentences.

1. Do the farmers work well together? Explain why or why not.

____

____

2. So far, Bean's plans have not worked out well. Why not?

____

____

Vocabulary Match the words on the left with its meaning on the right with a straight line.

1	declared		made a promise	A
2	swore a solemn oath		ill looking	B
3	snatch		to grab quickly away	C
4	miserable		said something out loud	D
5	sickly		not happy	E
6	hatchets		to look at something non-stop	F
7	staring		small axes	G
8	pistol		a hand gun	H

Chapters Seven to Eight

1. Fill in each blank with the correct word(s) from the chapters.

a) At _______ o'clock in the evening, Bean switched off the _________ of the tractor and climbed down from the driver's seat. __________ did the same. Both men had had enough.

b) They were tired and stiff from ____________ the tractors all day. They were also __________.

c) Bean's face was __________ with rage.

d) "Did you hear that, Mr Fox!" yelled Bean, bending low and _____________ down the hole. "It's not over yet, Mr Fox! We're not going home till we've strung you up dead as a ____________!"

e) Whereupon the three men all __________ hands with one another and swore a _________ oath that they would not go back to _________ farms until the fox was __________.

f) "What's the next move?" asked Bunce, the ___________ dwarf.

g) "Then there's only one thing to do," he said. "We _______ him out. We _________ here day and night watching the hole." So Boggis and Bunce and Bean sent ___________ down to their farms asking for __________, sleeping-bags and supper.

h) When darkness fell, they put on the caterpillar's ____________ . ________ men surround the hill all night, to keep the foxes from escaping.

i) Every so often, Mr Fox would _________ a little closer towards the _________ of the tunnel and take a sniff. Then he'd creep back and say, "They're still there."

Chapters Seven to Eight

Answer each question with a full sentence.

1. After three days and three nights, describe how the foxes were feeling.

____

2. Do the farmers come up with a good solution to keep the foxes from digging out? Explain.

____

____

3. Things look very bad for the Fox family. What do you think they can do to escape?

____

4. There are a lot of words in these chapters that use an apostrophe (').
For example: We're, it's, we'll, they're. Explain what the apostrophe does and how it is used.

____

____

5. Alliteration is when a set of words in a sentence all start with the same letter or sound. For example: "The big band played the bass." In this example, the letter "B" is repeated. Find a quote from the story that uses alliteration.

____

In these Chapters, Bean was 'purple with rage'. Have you ever been that angry? Describe what happened. If not, have you ever seen anyone that angry? What advice would you tell someone to help them control their temper?

Chapters Nine to Ten

Answer the questions in full sentences.

1. "This made it quite impossible for a fox or *indeed any other animal* to escape from the hill." What other animals might live there?

____

____

2. Are things as bad as they can get? Do you think there is anything worse that could happen?

____

____

Vocabulary Fit the words below into the provided groups. If you need help, use a dictionary.

dash	undefeated	marvelous	peek	ducked	prancing
Hallelujah	trough	lapped	plumpest	flick	jiffy
plank	cautiously	wearily	creaky	poked	courageous

Ways to MOVE or ACT (verbs)	PEOPLE, PLACES or THINGS (nouns)
DESCRIPTIONS of Ways to MOVE or ACT (adverbs)	**DESCRIPTIONS of PEOPLE, PLACES or THINGS (adjectives)**

Chapters Nine to Ten

1. Complete each sentence with a word from the list.

planks	break	excitement	three
face	digging	jumped	

a) The foxes were stuck in their hole for ____________ days.

b) The fox children beg "Couldn't we make a __________ for it?" Mrs Fox said, "I refuse to let you go up there and __________ those guns."

c) There was a little spark of ____________ dancing in the eyes of Mr Fox, because he had an idea.

d) "It won't work," Mr Fox said because it means more ___________. The young foxes ____________ up and cried that they could dig even more.

e) When Mr Fox was done digging, what was above the foxes head?
____

2. Number the events from ❶ to ❻ in the order they occurred in these chapters.

- **a)** Mr Fox lifted the plank up and saw chickens.

- **b)** He sent a little fox back to the Mother Fox with some chickens.

- **c)** The little foxes chased the chickens.

- **d)** Mr Fox asked his children to dig just a little bit more.

- **e)** Mr Fox suddenly got an idea.

- **f)** The foxes had a drink of water.

Chapters Nine to Ten

Answer each question with a full sentence.

1. How does Mr Fox get his children to want to dig after 3 days and 3 nights without any food or water?

____

2. Find a quote in Chapter 9 that shows that Mr Fox really loves and admires his children.

____

____

3. Why do you think Mr Fox would not tell his children where they were going? Give 2 reasons.

____

____

4. How is the way Mr Fox solves problems different than how the farmers solve problems?

____

____

5. Why does Mr Fox send one of the little foxes back to Mrs Fox with the chickens? Give 2 reasons.

____

____

The foxes keep digging and digging even though they are tired, hungry and thirsty. What could you do to keep going even when you are tired hungry or thirsty? Think of a time when you were too tired to continue something important. What did you do?

Chapters Eleven to Twelve

Answer the questions in complete sentences.

1. At the end of Chapter 10, Mr Fox tells one of his little foxes to take the chickens back to Mrs Fox. He says, "...the rest of us will be along in a jiffy, as soon as we have made a few other little arrangements." What do you think these little arrangements are?

    ____

    ____

2. Describe the relationship with the Fox family. How do they show they care about each other?

    ____

    ____

Vocabulary **Complete each sentence with a word from the list.**

exploding	bursting	spluttered	teased
tunneled	chaos	plucking	churgle

1. She called him names and __________ him about his hair.

2. The soap bubbles were __________ when they hit the ground.

3. The engine ran out of gas and ____________ to a stop.

4. The fireworks were ____________ with light in the air.

5. They began to dig and __________ right underneath the wall.

6. He started __________ the feathers off the turkey.

7. He tried to keep from laughing out loud, and it came out as a __________.

8. Everything was out of control. It was total __________!

Chapters Eleven to Twelve

1. Put a check mark (✓) next to the answer that is most correct.

a) The little fox hurried back to his mom feeling very:
- ○ **A** proud.
- ○ **B** hungry.
- ○ **C** happy.
- ○ **D** nervous.

b) When the little fox came back, his mom thought the chicken was:
- ○ **A** stolen.
- ○ **B** part of a dream.
- ○ **C** a toy.
- ○ **D** from Badger.

c) Who did Mr Fox meet when he left Chicken House Number One?
- ○ **A** Rabbit
- ○ **B** Mole
- ○ **C** Weasel
- ○ **D** Badger

d) Mr Fox admits that the situation is his fault and offers the feast to the other animals in apology. What does this show about Mr Fox?
- ○ **A** He is kind.
- ○ **B** He is guilty.
- ○ **C** He is proud.
- ○ **D** He is resentful.

e) When Badger helps to dig, what does his son do?
- ○ **A** He digs too.
- ○ **B** He gets the others.
- ○ **C** He sleeps.
- ○ **D** He eats chickens.

Chapters Eleven to Twelve

Answer each question with a full sentence.

1. Mrs Fox thinks Mr Fox is fantastic. Is she right? JUSTIFY her belief. Explain why she believes him to be fantastic.

   ____

   ____

   ____

2. Why did Mr Badger get lost?

   ____

   ____

3. Compare Mr Badger's and Mr Fox's responses to the problem they are facing. How does Mr Badger deal with the problem? How does Mr Fox deal with the problem?

   ____

   ____

   ____

   ____

4. Why does Mr Fox invite everyone to a feast?

   ____

   ____

The author of the story—Roald Dahl—believed it was important to help others, just like Mr Fox did. Think of a time when you helped someone with a problem they were having. What did you do? If not, what could you do to help other people in your family, school or community?

NAME: ___________________

Chapters Thirteen to Fourteen

Answer the questions in full sentences.

1. Mr Badger and his family will get something good from working with Mr Fox, but does Mr Fox get anything from Badger?

____

____

2. What is the next step in Mr Fox's plan?

____

____

Vocabulary Match the words on the left with its meaning on the right with a straight line.

1	saliva		feeling faint	A
2	overwhelmed		little bites	B
3	frump		food	C
4	morsels		out of style	D
5	grub		drool	E
6	swipe		said	F
7	proclaimed		take quickly	G
8	laid		placed	H
9	loot		stolen goods	I
10	heap		big pile	J

Chapters Thirteen to Fourteen

1. **Number the events from ❶ to ❻ in the order they were said in these chapters.**

☐ **a)** "There's nothing wrong with being respectable," Badger said.

☐ **b)** "I know my way around these farms blindfold." — Mr Fox

☐ **c)** "I'm mad about bacon!" cried Badger.

☐ **d)** "Now who in the world would build a wall under the ground?" asked Badger.

☐ **e)** "Don't talk about it, *please*," said Mr Fox. "It's a painful subject."

☐ **f)** "But what you don't know is which *part* of Bean's place we are about to visit."— Mr Fox

2. **Which characters said the following in these chapters?**

a) "Foxy," he said, "I love you." — ___________

b) "Don't be a twerp," said ___________

c) "And carrots, Dad." — ___________

d) "This is my party, so I shall do the choosing." — ___________

NAME: _______________

Chapters Thirteen to Fourteen

Answer each question with a full sentence.

1. Why doesn't Mr Fox want to talk about his tail?

2. "We are, in fact, directly underneath the most interesting part of that farm," Mr Fox says. Why is this part of the farm so interesting?

3. List all the types of food stored in Bunce's store house.

4. Why did Mr Fox call his son a 'twerp'? What does this show us about both Mr Fox and his son?

5. Why does Mr Badger feel bad about taking the food from the farmers? Where would Badgers normally get their food?

Stealing is wrong for humans. Is it ok for animals? Why or why not? Explain your thinking.

Chapters Fifteen to Sixteen

Answer the questions in full sentences.

1. So far, who has suffered the most because of the farmer's actions? Why?

   ____

   ____

2. At the very end of the last Chapter, Mr Fox had arrived at "the wall of an underground room." What do you think is inside this room?

   ____

   ____

Vocabulary Circle the correct word that matches the meaning of the underlined word.

1. A **sharp** face with whiskers.'

   a) good looking   **b)** pointy   **c)** like a knife   **d)** dangerous

2. 'You **saucy** beast.'

   a) gooey   **b)** fabulous   **c)** impertinent **d)** mean

3. 'This is my private **pitch**.'

   a) land   **b)** glue   **c)** secret   **d)** game

4. "Damp, gloomy **cellar**.'

   a) salesman   **b)** basement **c)** house   **d)** mood

5. The cider is "**Tremendous!**"

   a) great   **b)** horrible   **c)** bitter   **d)** huge

Chapters Fifteen to Sixteen

1.   Put a check mark (✓) next to the answer that is most correct.

a) Why did Rat tell Mr Fox to leave?
- ○ **A** He was there first.
- ○ **B** He didn't want to share.
- ○ **C** They were too noisy.
- ○ **D** The fox might eat him.

b) What does Badger say the cider was like?
- ○ **A** Fiery liquor.
- ○ **B** Miraculous.
- ○ **C** Fabulous.
- ○ **D** Like drinking sunbeams.

c) What danger was Mr Fox in while in the cider cellar?
- ○ **A** Rat was drunk.
- ○ **B** Being caught.
- ○ **C** Getting trapped.
- ○ **D** Being squished by a cider jar.

d) What did the woman in the cellar want?
- ○ **A** The fox's tail.
- ○ **B** To drink the cider.
- ○ **C** To poison the rats.
- ○ **D** Bean to come home.

e) As he left, what did Mr Fox say to Rat?
- ○ **A** Poppycock!
- ○ **B** Thanks!
- ○ **C** Bandits!
- ○ **D** You are going to be poisoned!

Chapters Fifteen to Sixteen

Answer each question with a full sentence.

1. How does Mr Fox convince Rat to let them in the cellar?

____

____

2. "Take a good look round," said Mr Fox. "Don't you see anything that interests you?" What were they expecting? What did they find?

____

____

3. Why did the animals get so excited about cider?

____

____

4. A simile is a comparison between two different things using 'like' or 'as'. For example, in Chapter 3: "Mr Fox was *quick as a whip*."; in Chapter 7, "Boggis said Mr Fox would be *dead as a dingbat*." Find a simile in Chapter 15 where Badger compares cider to 3 different things.

____

____

5. Why is it funny that the Rat shrieked: "Thieves, Robbers, Bandits and Burglars"?

____

____

Mr Fox says the cider will make the feast a banquet. Describe a special meal or celebration you have experienced with your family and/or friends. Paint a detailed picture of the event.

Chapters Seventeen to Eighteen

Answer the questions in full sentences.

1. The plot is the main storyline. What event started the struggle in this story?

   ____

   ____

2. What was the peak of the story, when the story was the most exciting?

   ____

   ____

3. What do you think will happen at the end of this story?

   ____

   ____

Vocabulary **Circle the correct word that matches the meaning of the underlined word.**

1. What a **glorious** day!

   a) nasty   **b)** beautiful   **c)** busy   **d)** boring

2. He was **famished**.

   a) ravenous   **b)** mean   **c)** alone   **d)** tired

3. "What an **impudent** young man!"

   a) polite   **b)** small   **c)** frightened   **d)** rude

4. He let out a huge **belch**.

   a) rat   **b)** groan   **c)** burp   **d)** chuckle

5. It was a **colossal** building full of cider!

   a) huge   **b)** stone   **c)** cold   **d)** dirty

After You Read 

Chapters Seventeen to Eighteen

1. **Circle** **T** if the statement is **TRUE** or **F** if it is **FALSE**.

   T F **a)** All rats drink too much and have bad tempers.

   T F **b)** Mr Fox's song shows he is concerned for his wife.

   T F **c)** The dining room seated more than 30 people.

   T F **d)** Everyone waited for Mr Fox to return before eating.

   T F **e)** Mr Fox dedicated the meal to the 3 farmers.

   T F **f)** "Better out than in," said Badger about Fox's belch.

2. **Complete the paragraph by filling in each blank with the correct word from the Chapters.**

"Let us think of tomorrow and the next day and the days after that. If we go out, we will be __________. Right?"
        a

    "But who wants to go out, anyway; let me ask you that? We are all __________, every one of us. We hate the outside. The outside is full of
  b

__________. We only go out because we have to, to get __________ for
 c   **d**

our families. But now, my friends, we have an entirely new __________. We
                                                           e

have a safe __________ leading to three of the finest __________ in the world."
             f   **g**

    "I therefore invite you all," Mr Fox went on, "to stay here with me __________."
   h

Chapters Seventeen to Eighteen

Answer each question with a full sentence.

1. Describe the underground tunnel system that Mr Fox dug.

____

____

2. What does the group see when they get back to the Fox's den?

____

____

3. What event shows that the Foxes will survive? Explain your answer.

____

____

4. Why did everyone toast Mr Fox?

____

5. The Farmers tried to harm Mr Fox, but ended up making his life much better. Write 3 ways that Mr Fox's life is better.

____

____

____

Journaling Prompt

In the end, the animals have created a great place to live and raise their families. Describe your perfect city, with everything you need to feel safe and happy.

Chapter 1

Hyperbole

Hyperbole is a huge exaggeration of a person. Usually it makes us laugh. Roald Dahl uses Hyperbole to describe the farmers in Chapter 1. Can you think of a person from a nursery rhyme or children's story? Write out some descriptions of the person. What did he or she look like? What did he or she do? What did he or she think about? Now, make the descriptions crazy or ridiculous. Remember to exaggerate. For example, "He was small: He was smaller than an ant." Write a paragraph of that character with the exaggerations.

Chapter 6

News Reporter

In Chapter 6, the town's people jeer at the farmers as they dig up the ground to try to get the foxes. Imagine you are a news reporter. Make up 10 questions that you would ask the farmers about what they are doing. Write it up and include the answers the farmers would give to those questions.

Chapter 10

Point of View

In Chapter 10, the Author wrote the 'stupid chickens'. In this book the foxes are the 'good guys' and the farmers are the 'bad guys'. In the real world, many people think that foxes are pests. Farmers don't like foxes because they eat the farm animals. The farm animals, like chickens, are the victims. Instead, in the book we see the world from the point of view of Mr Fox. Chickens, from the foxes' point of view, are 'stupid'. Imagine other 'villains or pests' in the real world: mosquitoes, skunks, rats, sharks, Tyrannosaurus Rex or others. Write a short story told from the perspective of one of these pests. Tell about how they need to survive and feed their family.

Chapter 14

Courtroom Defense

In Chapter 14, Mr Badger feels bad that they are stealing. Imagine that Mr Fox was facing a Judge in Court and had to defend himself for taking from the farmers. What would Mr Fox say to the judge? Base your answer on facts from the whole book including Chapter 14. Think of at least 3 reasons Mr Fox would use to defend himself.

Chapter 17

Rhymes

In Chapter 17 (and Chapter 1), the characters sing a little rhyme about what is happening in the story. These little rhymes are 5 lines long and follow a pattern. The first line, second line and last line (fifth line) all rhyme with each other. Lines 3 and 4 don't rhyme with lines 1,2 and 5, but they do rhyme with each other. Now it is your turn: write a rhyme about one event or person in the story. Use the same pattern. (Writing hint: think of the topic and write one line. Then, brainstorm as many words that you can think of that rhymes with the last word in your topic sentence. This can make it easier to write a rhyme).

Chapter 18

Memoir

Imagine it is many years after the story is over. One of the little Foxes is all grown up. He decides to write a memoir. (A memoir is a story about the important moments in your life.) The little Fox writes about the time in his life when his father earned the nickname "Fantastic Mr Fox." What would he remember? What would he think would be important to write about? Write little Fox's memoir. Be sure to write at least 4 things his father did that was fantastic.

NAME: ______________

Word Search Puzzle

Find the words from the story. The words are written across, down, on an angle, and some are written backwards.

cellar	desperate	jeered	obstinate	solemn
crater	famished	lousy	prancing	spluttered
creep	fantastic	maniac	ravenous	staring
dash	furious	mean	refuse	starving
decent	impudent	oath	shrieked	undefeated

f	n	u	i	t	n	e	d	u	p	m	i	y	x	r			
f	a	m	i	s	h	e	d	a	c	d	f	t	a	a			
s	q	n	s	v	d	q	t	y	b	d	g	r	v	t			
o	b	s	t	i	n	a	t	e	e	e	h	j	e	l			
l	l	x	a	a	i	y	s	a	c	r	e	e	p	z			
e	s	m	r	a	s	l	t	h	q	e	t	u	r	p			
m	u	t	v	e	n	t	o	e	n	e	n	i	a	u			
n	o	o	i	v	d	b	i	u	e	j	e	t	n	b			
f	i	p	n	q	v	h	d	c	s	h	c	d	c	c			
x	r	r	g	o	v	e	a	e	u	y	e	o	i	g			
l	u	e	a	p	k	i	o	l	f	f	d	i	n	a			
s	f	t	z	e	n	g	n	l	e	z	t	y	g	v			
f	h	a	i	a	j	s	t	a	r	i	n	g	w	c			
r	x	r	m	e	a	n	t	r	n	s	a	r	t	u			
a	h	c	r	a	v	e	n	o	u	s	g	h	b	c			
s	r	t	v	l	d	e	s	p	e	r	a	t	e	w			
d	e	r	e	t	t	u	l	p	s	m	p	q	a	x			

Comprehension Quiz

31

Answer each question with a full sentence.

1. How are the farmers the same and how are they different?

____

____ **4**

2. Why did Bean make all the plans for the farmers?

____ **1**

3. List 3 of Bean's plans to kill the fox.

____

____ **3**

4. Why did Bean's plans all fail? Give 2 reasons.

____

____ **2**

5. Why does the author use exaggeration to describe the farmers?
Give 2 reasons.

____

____ **2**

6. Mr Fox is a careful hunter. Name 3 useful hunting skills he used to
outsmart the farmers at the beginning of the story.

____

____ **3**

7. Why are the little foxes present in the story? Use a fact from the
story to explain your answer.

____

____ **2**

SUBTOTAL: **/17**

   Fantastic Mr Fox CC2316

NAME: ___________________

Comprehension Quiz

8. What is Mrs Fox's 'job' in this story? Name 2 things she does that are important to the story.

_______________________________________ **2**

____

9. Compare Mr Fox to Mr Badger. How do they react to being trapped underground by the farmers?

_______________________________________ **2**

____

10. What is the climax of the story?

_______________________________________ **1**

____

11. What are Mr Fox's plans for long-term survival? Include 2 details that show he wasn't just thinking about escaping the farmers.

_______________________________________ **2**

____

12. If you could ask Mr Fox, "What is the secret to a good plan?" What do you think he would say?

_______________________________________ **1**

13. The farmers' plans didn't work. Name 3 bad side effects.

_______________________________________ **3**

____

14. This story is called, "Fantastic Mr Fox". What are 3 fantastic things that Mr Fox did in the story?

_______________________________________ **3**

____

SUBTOTAL: **/14**

11

1.
Answers will vary.

Vocabulary

1. disgusting

2. smothered

3. enormously

4. beastly; nasty

5. crooks

6. pot-bellied

7. cleverest

12

1.
a) A

b) D

c) B

d) C

e) B

13

1.
The children sang that one was fat, one was short and one was lean. They were all crooks and all mean.

2.
"This was because he ate three boiled chickens smothered in dumplings every day for breakfast, lunch and supper."

3.
He ate doughnuts mashed with goose livers. "This diet gave him a tummy ache and a beastly temper."

4.
"Farmer Bean never ate any food at all. Instead he drank gallons of strong cider."

5.
The farmers were so mean because they were unhealthy from the food they ate, and the drink they drank, and maybe because they had too much.

14

1.
Answers will vary.

2.
Answers will vary.

3.
Answers will vary.

Vocabulary

1. B

2. A

3. C

4. G

5. H

6. D

7. E

8. F

15

1.
a) F

b) T

c) F

d) T

e) F

f) F

g) F

h) T

2.
a) hoping

b) decent

c) hole

16

1.
A hole in the ground under a big tree on a hill in a wood.

2.
He asked Mrs Fox what she would like for dinner.

3.
The farmers sat on their own farms in the dark with their guns.

4.
Mr Fox approached from downwind. He smelled where the farmers were hiding.

5.
They are greedy.

6.
"You've never had a decent plan yet," said Bunce.

Vocabulary

Across

2. poisonous

6. rustling

8. murky

10. doze

12. scrape

Down

1. cocky

2. pricked

3. scrunch

4. tattered

5. twitched

7. glint

9. reeks

11. crouched

13. phew

1.

a) chicken-skins; goose-livers; apple cider

b) shone; tattered

c) dozed; stump

d) crunch; ceiling; awful; electric

2.

a) 2

b) 6

c) 1

d) 3

e) 4

f) 5

1.

"Yes, but just don't get careless," said Mrs Fox. "You know they'll be waiting for you, all three of them."

2.

Answers will vary, but may include: Mr Fox doesn't want anyone to find their home. He wanted to keep it secret to protect his family.

3.

Mr Fox used his ears, his eyes and his nose.

4.

He is very 'glum' or saddened by the loss of his tail.

5.

She loves him, he heard the noise and warned them and he thought of a way to keep them alive.

6.

Mrs Fox wanted to protect her children and hugged them tight when they were scared. They all dug together. They praised and encouraged each other.

1.

Mrs. Fox thought he was fantastic because he didn't panic, and he had thought of a plan to save the family.

2.

Answers will vary.

3.

Answers will vary.

Vocabulary

1. a

2. b

3. b

4. c

1.

a) T

b) F

c) T

d) F

e) F

f) F

g) F

h) T

i) F

2.

a) ✓ B

b) ✓ C

1.

Because they dug all day and all night.

2.

He said it was a rotten idea.

3.

Answers will vary, but may include: They can't think of their own ideas.

4.

They have destroyed the wood and the hill.

5.

Answers will vary, but may include: It is a race for survival for the foxes to out-dig the mechanical diggers. It is a race to get the fox for the farmers.

23

1.
Answers will vary.

2.
Answers will vary.

Vocabulary

1. D

2. A

3. C

4. E

5. B

6. G

7. F

8. H

24

1.

a) six; motor; Bunce

b) driving; hungry

c) purple

d) shouting; dingbat

e) shook; solemn; their; caught

f) pot-bellied

g) starve; camp; messages; tents

h) headlamps; 108

i) creep; mouth

25

1.
Starving and desperate.

2.
Not really: their farms are shut down with all their employees guarding the hill. Also, if the fox dug so deep already, what's stopping him from digging farther?

3.
Answers will vary, but may include: Dig farther.

4.
Answers will vary, but may include: The apostrophe replaces a missing word. "We are" = "We're"; "it is" = "it's"; "we will" = "we'll"; and "they are" = "they're".

5.
Answers will vary, but may include: "Bean made a sickly smile. When he smiled you saw his scarlet gums."

26

1.
Answers will vary, but may include: moles, mice, rabbits, weasels, grouse, porcupine, badgers.

2.
Answers will vary.

Vocabulary

Verbs:
dash, peek, ducked, prancing, lapped, flick, poked

Nouns:
trough, plank, Hallelujah, jiffy

Adverbs:
cautiously, wearily

Adjectives:
creaky, plumpest, marvelous, undefeated, courageous

27

1.

a) three

b) break; face

c) excitement

d) digging; jumped

e) planks

2.

a) 3

b) 6

c) 4

d) 2

e) 1

f) 5

28

1.
He suggests that they can't do it.

2.
"Mr Fox looked at the four Small Foxes and he smiled. What fine children I have, he thought. They are starving to death and haven't had a drink for three days, but they are still undefeated."

3.
Answers will vary, but may include: So they would keep digging calmly and steadily, and to avoid disappointment if he didn't reach the chicken house right away.

4.
Mr Fox tries to stay calm; the farmers act out in anger. Mr Fox thinks things through and plans ahead; the farmers just react to each situation.

5.
Answers will vary, but may include: He gets the chickens back to Mrs Fox so she won't be discouraged or worried, and so she can start preparing dinner for them and they will eat that much quicker.

EZ✓

Column 1 — page 29

1.
Answers will vary.

2.
Answers will vary, but may include: Mr Fox encourages and praises his children and thinks of his wife's needs before his own.

Vocabulary

1. teased
2. bursting
3. spluttered
4. exploding
5. tunneled
6. plucking
7. churgle
8. chaos

Column 2 — page 30

1.
a) ✓ C

b) ✓ B

c) ✓ D

d) ✓ A

e) ✓ B

Column 3 — page 31

1.
Answers will vary, but may include: Mr Fox is fantastic because he feeds his family, protects them, keeps calm under crisis, solves problems, and is generous to the other animals.

2.
Mr Badger is not used to having to stay underground. He isn't used to hunting at the farms each night.

3.
Mr Badger digs and gets lost, and then gives up. Mr Fox sits and thinks things through, then follows his plan.

4.
Answers will vary, but may include: He feels responsible for the farmers attack on the hill. He is also kind and generous.

Column 4 — page 32

1.
Answers will vary, but may include: Yes. Badger is a terrific digger.

2.
Answers will vary, but may include: Probably to visit the other two farms.

Vocabulary

1. E
2. A
3. D
4. B
5. C
6. G
7. F
8. H
9. I
10. J

Column 5 — page 33

1.
a) 5
b) 2
c) 3
d) 6
e) 1
f) 4

2.
a) Mr Badger

b) Mr Fox

c) smallest fox

d) Mr Fox

Column 6 — page 34

1.
It reminds him of the danger they are in. Also, he is sad he lost his tail.

2.
He knows it's where the best food is kept.

3.
Ducks, geese, hams, bacon, and carrots.

4.
Answers will vary, but may include: He thinks his son is not thinking when he says 'and carrots too.' They joke around and also the son is very thoughtful and the father appreciates that.

5.
Answers will vary, but may include: Mr Badger is used to hunting in the woods for rodents and insects and he wouldn't normally steal from the farmers.

1.

Answers will vary.

2.

Answers will vary.

Vocabulary

1. b

2. c

3. a

4. b

5. a

35

1.

a) ✓ B

b) ✓ D

c) ✓ B

d) ✓ A

e) ✓ B

36

1.

He threatened to eat him.

2.

They were thinking it would be turkeys. They found cider.

3.

They have had turkeys a lot, but they wouldn't have had cider very much.

4.

Cider is like: liquid gold, drinking sunbeams, and rainbows.

5.

Answers will vary, but may include: It's ironic. The rat who is stealing the farmer's cider calls Mr Fox a thief, robber, bandit and burglar.

37

1.

Answers will vary, but may include: The farmers shoot off Mr Fox's tail.

2.

Answers will vary, but may include: The farmers camp around the hole in the crater.

3.

Answers will vary.

Vocabulary

1. b

2. a

3. d

4. c

5. a

38

1.

a) F

b) T

c) T

d) F

e) T

f) T

2.

a) killed

b) diggers

c) enemies

d) food

e) set-up

f) tunnel

g) stores

h) forever

39

1.

The tunnel runs from Bean's Cellar, to Bunce's store house, to Boggis' Chicken house number one, and then down to Mr Fox's home.

2.

A huge new dining hall has been created and all the diggers are there feasting.

3.

Answers will vary, but may include: The feast and invitation to live together.

4.

It was his plan and his skills that got them out of the trouble they were in.

5.

Answers will vary, but may include: Mr Fox and his family don't have to go out for food anymore, they have easy access to the food supplies, and they have lots of new friends.

40

Word Search Puzzle

f	n	u	i	t	n	e	d	u	p	m	i	y	x	r
f	a	m	i	s	h	e	d	a	c	d	f	t	a	a
s	q	n	s	v	d	q	t	y	b	d	g	r	v	t
o	b	s	t	i	n	a	t	e	e	e	h	j	e	l
l	l	x	a	a	i	y	s	a	c	r	e	e	p	z
e	s	m	r	a	s	l	t	h	q	e	t	u	r	p
m	u	t	v	e	n	t	o	e	n	e	n	i	g	u
n	o	o	i	v	d	b	i	u	e	j	e	t	n	b
f	i	p	n	q	v	h	d	c	s	h	c	d	c	c
x	r	r	g	o	v	e	a	e	u	y	e	o	i	g
l	u	e	a	p	k	i	o	l	f	f	d	i	n	a
s	f	t	z	e	n	g	n	l	e	z	t	y	g	v
f	h	a	i	a	j	s	t	a	r	i	n	g	w	c
r	x	r	m	e	a	n	t	r	n	s	a	r	t	u
a	h	c	r	a	v	e	n	o	u	s	g	h	b	c
s	r	t	v	l	d	e	s	p	e	r	a	t	e	w
d	e	r	e	t	t	u	l	p	s	m	p	q	a	x

1.

Answers will vary, but may include: They are all mean, greedy, have a terrible diet, hate the fox, and rush into action without thinking. Boggis is a chicken farmer, Bunce is the duck and goose farmer, and Bean is the turkey and apple cider farmer.

2.

He was the only one who could think of plans.

3.

Answers will vary, but may include: Shoot him at his home when he leaves, dig him out, and starve him out.

4.

Answers will vary, but may include: He didn't think them through and they just rushed into action.

5.

Answers will vary, but may include: To make the farmers look more ridiculous/villainous and to make the reader laugh.

6.

Answers will vary, but may include: move cautiously, listen carefully and approach downwind.

7.

The little foxes help their father to work his plan. They show their father's character as a loving father and fantastic fox.

8.

Answers will vary, but may include: Mrs Fox points out her husband's qualities.

9.

Answers will vary, but may include: Mr Fox thinks of a plan to get food; he digs the tunnels to the right places; he doesn't give up and encourages his children. Mr Badger digs around lost and gives up.

10.

The climax is when the fox family is surrounded and the children want to make a break for it.

11.

He digs the tunnels to the farms but replaces the floor boards/bricks so that no one would know they had been there.

12.

Answers will vary, but may include: Think it through.

13.

Answers will vary, but may include: They ruined the woods, they made everyone laugh at them, and they aren't working their farms.

14.

Answers will vary, but may include: He provided for his family, he didn't give up, and he saved them from the farmers.

Character Sketch

What does Mr Fox think about? What does he hear? What does he see? What are his weaknesses?... Using the drawing of a fox below, find facts from the book that tell you about Mr Fox.

Fantastic Mr Fox CC2316

Summary Sentence Sandwich

Students will easily organize their facts from the story into a topic sentence, layers of detail, and concluding sentence with this summary sentence sandwich graphic organizer. Students will write their topic sentence on the top bread, details supporting their topic on the tomato, lettuce, meat, and cheese, then finally their conclusion on the bottom bread.

Topic Sentence:_______________________________

____

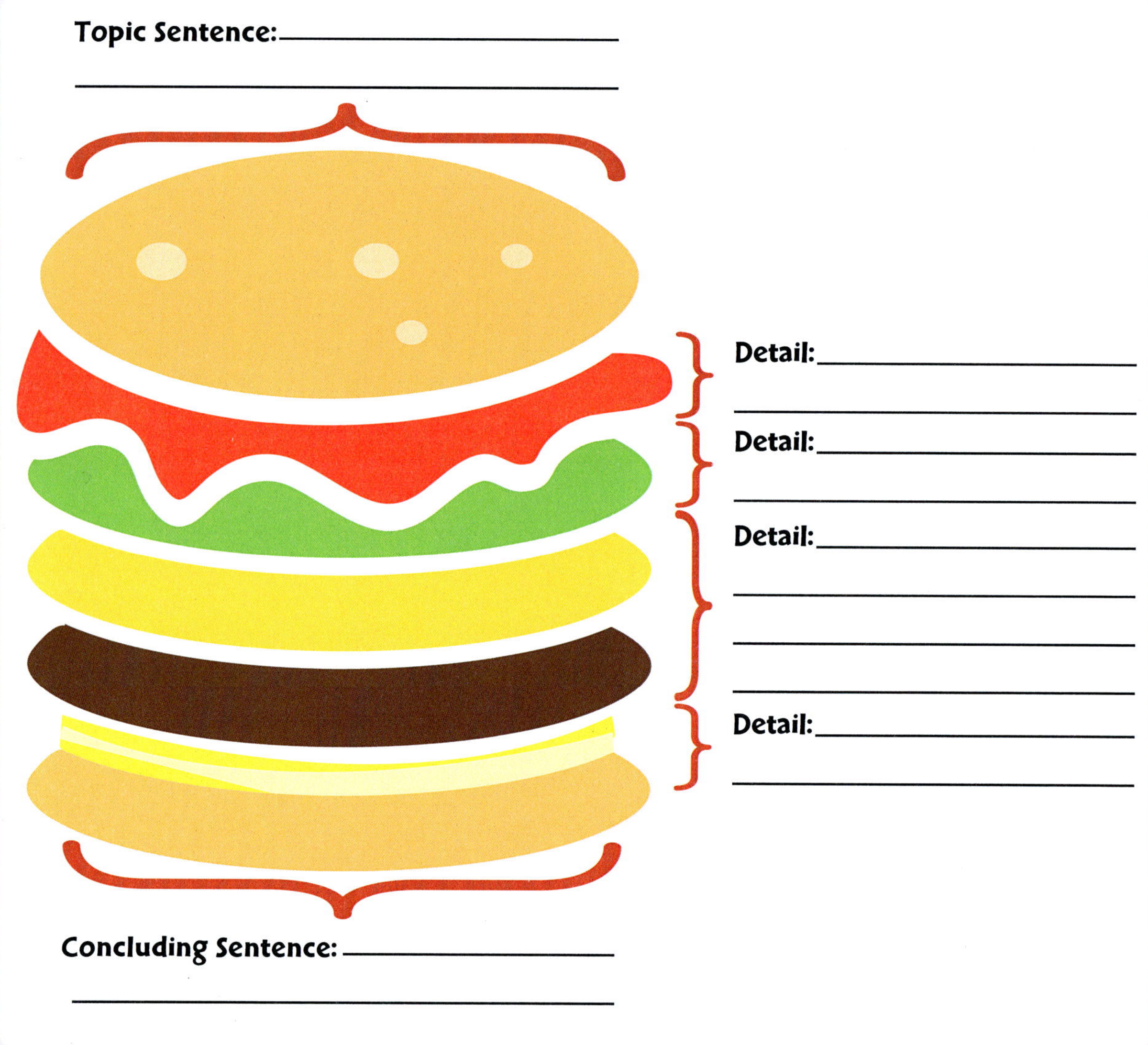

Detail:_______________________________

____

Detail:_______________________________

____

Detail:_______________________________

____

____

____

Detail:_______________________________

____

Concluding Sentence: _______________________________

____

Plot Diagram

Students will gather the key points to plot development: introduction, rising action, climax, falling action, and conclusion. Students will write down quotes on the plot diagram to help them find facts in the story.

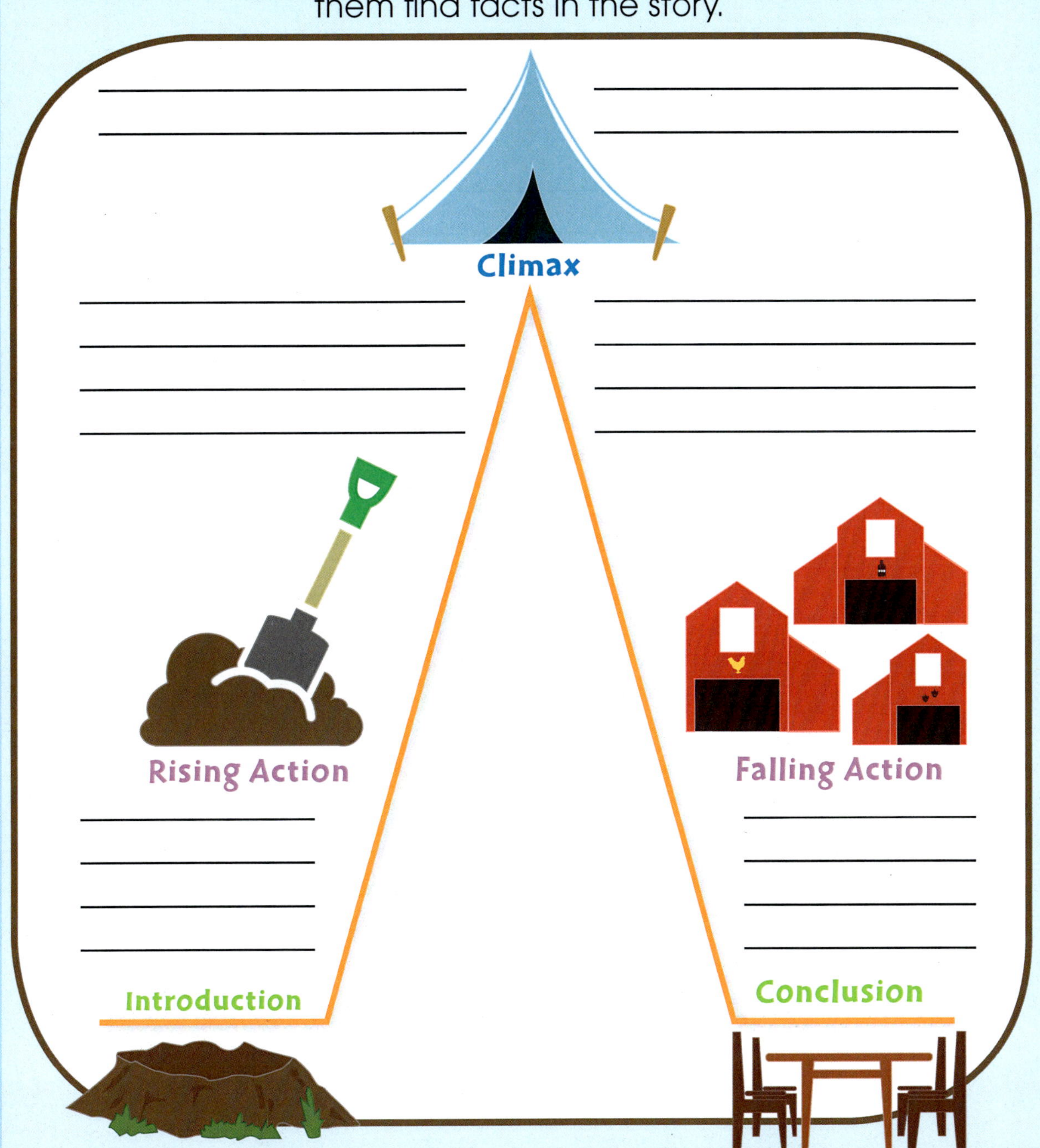

Fantastic Mr Fox CC2316

- **RSL.3.1** Ask and answer questions to demonstrate understanding of a text, referring explicitly to the text as the basis for the answers.
- **RSL.3.2** Recount stories, including fables, folktales, and myths from diverse cultures; determine the central message, lesson, or moral and explain how it is conveyed through key details in the text.
- **RSL.3.3** Describe characters in a story and explain how their actions contribute to the sequence of events.
- **RSL.3.4** Determine the meaning of words and phrases as they are used in a text, distinguishing literal from non-literal language.
- **RSL.3.5** Refer to parts of stories, dramas, and poems when writing or speaking about a text, using terms such as chapter, scene, and stanza; describe how each successive part builds on earlier sections.
- **RSL.3.6** Distinguish their own point of view from that of the narrator or those of the characters.
- **RSL.3.7** Explain how specific aspects of a text's illustrations contribute to what is conveyed by the words in a story.
- **RSL.3.10** By the end of the year read and comprehend literature, including stories, dramas, and poetry, at the high end of the grades 2–3 text complexity band independently and proficiently.
- **RSL.4.1** Refer to details and examples in a text when explaining what the text says explicitly and when drawing inferences from the text.
- **RSL.4.2** Determine a theme of a story, drama, or poem from details in the text; summarize the text.
- **RSL.4.3** Describe in depth a character, setting, or event in a story or drama, drawing on specific details in the text.
- **RSL.4.4** Determine the meaning of words and phrases as they are used in a text, including those that allude to significant characters found in mythology.
- **RSL.4.6** Compare and contrast the point of view from which different stories are narrated, including the difference between first- and third-person narrations.
- **RSL.4.10** By the end of the year read and comprehend literature, including stories, dramas, and poetry, in the grades 4–5 text complexity band proficiently, with scaffolding as needed at the high end of the range.
- **RSFS.3.3** Know and apply grade-level phonics and word analysis skills in decoding words. **A)** Identify and know the meaning of the most common prefixes and derivational suffixes. **B)** Decode words with common Latin suffixes. **C)** Decode multi-syllable words. d. Read grade-appropriate irregularly spelled words.
- **RSFS.3.4** Read with sufficient accuracy and fluency to support comprehension. **A)** Read grade-level text with purpose and understanding. **B).** Read grade-level prose and poetry orally with accuracy, appropriate rate, and expression on successive readings **C)** Use context to confirm or self-correct word recognition and understanding, rereading as necessary.
- **RSFS.4.3** Know and apply grade-level phonics and word analysis skills in decoding words. **A)** Use combined knowledge of all letter-sound correspondences, syllabication patterns, and morphology to read accurately unfamiliar multisyllabic words in context and out of context.
- **RSFS.4.4** Read with sufficient accuracy and fluency to support comprehension. **A)** Read grade-level text with purpose and understanding. **B)** Read grade-level prose and poetry orally with accuracy, appropriate rate, and expression on successive readings. **C)** Use context to confirm or self-correct word recognition and understanding, rereading as necessary.
- **WS.3.1** Write opinion pieces on topics or texts, supporting a point of view with reasons. **A)** Introduce the topic or text they are writing about, state an opinion, and create an organizational structure that lists reasons. **B)** Provide reasons that support the opinion. **C)** Use linking words and phrases to connect opinion and reasons. **D)** Provide a concluding statement or section.
- **WS.3.2** Write informative/explanatory texts to examine a topic and convey ideas and information clearly. **A)** Introduce a topic and group related information together; include illustrations when useful to aiding comprehension. **B)** Develop the topic with facts, definitions, and details. **C)** Use linking words and phrases to connect ideas within categories of information. **D)** Provide a concluding statement or section.
- **WS.3.3** Write narratives to develop real or imagined experiences or events using effective technique, descriptive details, and clear event sequences. **A)** Establish a situation and introduce a narrator and/or characters; organize an event sequence that unfolds naturally. **B)** Use dialogue and descriptions of actions, thoughts, and feelings to develop experiences and events or show the response of characters to situations. **C)** Use temporal words and phrases to signal event order. **D)** Provide a sense of closure.
- **WS.3.4** With guidance and support from adults, produce writing in which the development and organization are appropriate to task and purpose.
- **WS.3.7** Conduct short research projects that build knowledge about a topic.
- **WS.3.8** Recall information from experiences or gather information from print and digital sources; take brief notes on sources and sort evidence into provided categories.
- **WS.4.1** Write opinion pieces on topics or texts, supporting a point of view with reasons and information. **A)** Introduce a topic or text clearly, state an opinion, and create an organizational structure in which related ideas are grouped to support the writer's purpose. **B)** Provide reasons that are supported by facts and details. **C)** Link opinion and reasons using words and phrases. **D)** Provide a concluding statement or section related to the opinion presented.
- **WS.4.3** Write narratives to develop real or imagined experiences or events using effective technique, descriptive details, and clear event sequences. **A)** Orient the reader by establishing a situation and introducing a narrator and/or characters; organize an event sequence that unfolds naturally. **B)** Use dialogue and description to develop experiences and events or show the responses of characters to situations. **C)** Use a variety of transitional words and phrases to manage the sequence of events. **D)** Use concrete words and phrases and sensory details to convey experiences and events precisely. **E)** Provide a conclusion that follows from the narrated experiences or events.
- **WS.4.4** Produce clear and coherent writing in which the development and organization are appropriate to task, purpose, and audience.
- **WS.4.7** Conduct short research projects that build knowledge through investigation of different aspects of a topic.
- **WS.4.8** Recall relevant information from experiences or gather relevant information from print and digital sources; take notes and categorize information, and provide a list of sources.
- **WS.4.9** Draw evidence from literary or informational texts to support analysis, reflection, and research. **A)** Apply *grade 4 Reading standards* to literature. **B)** Apply *grade 4 Reading standards* to informational texts.